W9-CCF-261

3 1502 00757 3734

Y
363.3494
HAWKINS

8/17

Please check all items for damages
before leaving the Library.
Thereafter you will be held
responsible for all injuries
to items beyond reasonable wear.

Helen M. Plum Memorial Library

Lombard, Illinois

A daily fine will be charged for
overdue materials.

FEB   2013

TSUNAMI DISASTERS

John Hawkins

rosen publishing's
rosen
central®

HELEN PLUM
LIBRARY
LOMBARD, IL

363.3494
NAW

This edition first published in 2012 by The Rosen Publishing Group, Inc.
29 East 21st Street, New York, NY 10010

Copyright © 2012 Arcturus Publishing Limited

All rights reserved. No part of this book may be reproduced in any form without permission in writing from the publisher, except by a reviewer.

Author: John Hawkins
Editors: Joe Harris and Penny Worms
Design: Graham Rich
Cover design: Graham Rich

Picture credits:
Corbis: cover, 7, 13, 16, 20, 23, 31, 40, 45tc, 45b. Getty: 14b, 18b, 24b, 26b, 35, 44t, 44tc, 44bc, 44b, 45t, 45c, 45bc. Rex Features: 5, 17, 42, 43. Science Photo Library: 1, 4, 8, 9, 10. Shutterstock: 12, 14t, 18t, 22, 24t, 26t, 28, 30, 33, 34, 36, 38t, 41, 44c. TopFoto: 32. U.S. Geological Survey: 6. Wikimedia: 38b.

Cover image: Natori, Miyagi Prefecture, northeastern Japan. A massive tsunami engulfs a residential area after a powerful earthquake, March 11, 2011.

Library of Congress Cataloging-in-Publication Data

Hawkins, John.
  Tsunami disasters / John Hawkins.
      p. cm. -- (Catastrophe!)
  Includes bibliographical references and index.
  ISBN 978-1-4488-6005-0 (library binding)
1. Tsunami--Juvenile literature. I. Title.
  GC221.5.H39 2012
  551.46'37--dc23

                                2011028534

Printed in China
SL001929US

CPSIA Compliance Information: Batch #W12YA. For further information, contact Rosen Publishing, New York, New York, at 1-800-237-9932.

3 1502 00757 3734

Contents

What Is a Tsunami?

A tsunami is a huge wave that can flood the land with devastating effects. Earthquakes under the ocean cause the majority of tsunamis. Landslides, volcanic eruptions, and even meteorites falling into the sea can cause others. Waves flow outward in a circle from the point where the disturbance happens—like ripples spreading from a stone dropped in a pond.

A tsunami can have devastating effects if it strikes an area where people live and work.

HARBOR WAVE

The word *tsunami* is Japanese for "harbor wave." It is an appropriate name, as it is when a tsunami hits a harbor or other populated coastal area that its destructive power is felt. It can flood towns and villages with little warning, destroying all in its path and killing people and animals. Then the wave retreats, sweeping things out to sea.

STARTING SMALL

Far out at sea, the tsunami is a tiny wave, but it can travel as fast as a commercial jet—over 466 mph (750 kph). The height of the wave may be only 2 feet (60 cm), and so it often goes unnoticed by ships in the area. As the tsunami approaches land and the water gets shallower, the wave slows down and grows taller. By the time it reaches the shore, it can be 100 feet (30 m) tall.

The ocean recedes from the coast of Kalutara, Sri Lanka, during the tsunami that struck in December 2004.

DEVASTATION

A tsunami can bring total devastation in just a few terrifying minutes. The most destructive tsunamis are those that strike without warning, as it takes most people only about 10 minutes to move to safety. In some cases, the sea draws back before the tsunami strikes. This is the wave pulling the sea into itself. There may be a hissing and cracking sound, or a rumble like thunder, as the tsunami approaches.

SPOT A TSUNAMI

	Normal wave	Tsunami
Speed	5–62 mph (8–100 kph)	500–620 mph (800–1,000 kph)
Wave period (time between waves)	5–20 seconds	10 minutes to 2 hours
Wave length (distance between waves)	328–656 ft (100–200 m)	62–310 miles (100–500 km)

The Tsunami Zone

Tsunamis can happen anywhere, but most occur around the Pacific Ocean. Volcanic eruptions and earthquakes are very common around the edges of the Pacific, both inland and just off the coast. These can trigger tsunamis that spread across the whole ocean.

EARTH'S JIGSAW

The surface, or crust, of the earth is divided into chunks called tectonic plates that fit together like a giant jigsaw puzzle. There are seven large plates and several smaller ones. Beneath the crust, semiliquid, red-hot rock moves very slowly, dragging the plates with it. At the joins between plates, they rub or push against each other. These are geologically active areas where earthquakes and volcanic eruptions happen.

THE PACIFIC

The Pacific Ocean sits on a vast single plate. Because of this, there are borders with other plates all the way around the ocean. Most of the boundary of the oceanic plate is vulnerable to earthquakes.

The red dots indicate volcanoes and earthquake zones around the Pacific. This is called the Ring of Fire.

A lone man watches the approach of the tsunami that swept him away on Hilo's Pier 1 in Hawaii in 1946.

LANDFALL

A tsunami can strike land a long way from the event that causes it—even on the other side of the ocean. In 1946, an earthquake off the coast of Alaska triggered a tsunami that struck the Hawaiian Islands in the middle of the Pacific Ocean five hours later. The earthquake was some 2,500 miles (4,000 km) from Hawaii. When a tsunami strikes a region that did not feel the earthquake, it can seem to come from nowhere. When one reaches the shore quickly and near the source of the earthquake or eruption, it brings new devastation to an area hit only minutes before.

 INLAND TSUNAMIS

Tsunamis can happen in an inland sea or lake. There have been many tsunamis in the Mediterranean Sea. Earthquakes and volcanic activity around Italy and Greece have caused some disastrous tsunamis through history, including some believed to have destroyed ancient Greek and Minoan cities thousands of years ago. Smaller bodies of water, like lakes and rivers, can also be affected by tsunamis. In 1811, a large earthquake struck New Madrid, Missouri, reversing the flow of the Mississippi River. The eruption of Mount St. Helens in Washington State in 1980 caused a tsunami on nearby Spirit Lake.

Earthquakes and Tsunamis

The earth's tectonic plates move slowly—about the same speed as your fingernails grow. But where they push or grind together, pressure can build up over years or centuries. When the tension becomes too great, the plates slip with a jolt, causing an earthquake. Over the last 2,000 years, earthquakes have caused more than 80 percent of the tsunamis in the Pacific.

EARTHQUAKE AREA

At the edges of the ocean, the oceanic plate pushes against the continental plates (plates carrying land). The oceanic plate is denser, so it is forced downward toward the hot mantle, where it melts. Earthquakes can occur when a plate snaps or springs back into place.

sinking oceanic plates

On the right of this diagram, an oceanic plate is pushed down below the edge of a continental plate. On the left, one oceanic plate is forced down by another.

FILLING THE GAP

When the earth's crust under the sea suddenly slips, a massive column of water may fall downward, rushing in to fill a gap, or water may be rapidly thrust upward. Because of gravity, the water immediately corrects itself to regain a smooth surface. As it does so, it sends out a series of massive waves.

LAND RIPPLES

If there is an earthquake on land but near the coast, ripples of energy, just like waves on water but moving more slowly, run through the solid ground. When they meet the sea, the waves are transferred to waves in the water. Some quite small earthquakes on land translate into gigantic and dangerous tsunamis.

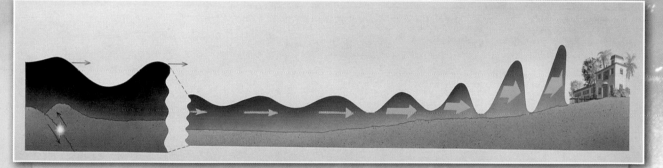

When it is far out to sea the tsunami is small but moves quickly. As it approaches shore, it slows down and grows much taller.

WHY DOES IT HAPPEN?

Why do waves get larger near land? The energy of a wave remains much the same, just dropping slightly as it travels. When it is out at sea, the energy is dispersed through the whole depth of the wave, but as the water becomes shallower near the coast, the water is forced upward as it becomes compressed.

Volcanoes and Tsunamis

The very same areas that are plagued by earthquakes also suffer volcanic eruptions. As the oceanic crust is forced downward, it melts underground. Some rises through the earth's upper layer to create vast magma chambers beneath volcanoes. When a volcano can hold no more, the magma is hurled out under pressure, making an eruption.

The Greek island of Thera (Santorini) as it may have looked before the volcano erupted (left) and as it looks now (right).

ERUPTION

Scalding molten rock explodes into the air, sometimes blowing away part of the volcano itself. When the magma chamber has emptied, the weight of the mountain above often comes crashing down into the empty space, causing the volcano to collapse inward.

WATER AND FIRE

If a volcano is on the coast, or forms an island in the sea, water and molten rock make an explosive mixture. Water rushing into the magma chamber often causes an explosion so violent the volcano is blown apart, and the sudden rush of a mass of water can cause a tsunami. A tsunami may also happen if huge rocks are thrown into the sea by an eruption.

SUBMERGED

Many volcanoes are completely underwater. An undersea eruption can force a column of water upward, or the sea floor can collapse into an emptying magma chamber. Either event can cause a tsunami.

COMBINED ASSAULT

Earth tremors—minor earthquakes—can be the first sign that a volcano is about to erupt. Either the earth tremors or the eruption itself can cause a tsunami, and often an area will be devastated by more than one disaster in a short period of time.

SANTORINI

The Minoan island of Thera, now known as Santorini in Greece, was a volcanic island that experienced a huge volcanic eruption some time between 1650 and 1450 BCE. The eruption caused the entire volcano to collapse in on itself and the sea rushed into the caldera (volcanic crater) causing tsunamis in the Aegean Sea. Many believe that the sinking of Thera was the origin of the legend of Atlantis, the great empire that disappeared into the depths of the sea.

Devastation in Japan, 2011

The Tohoku Earthquake of March 11, 2011, was the fifth most powerful earthquake in recorded history. The epicenter was approximately 80 miles (130 km) off the northeast coast of Japan, at a depth of only 20 miles (32 km). A tsunami warning was issued, but nothing prepared the country for what was about to happen.

QUAKE

The earthquake measured 9.0 on the Richter scale, the largest Japan had ever experienced. The violent tremors rocked buildings in Tokyo, over 230 miles (370 km) away. The damage was bad but not disastrous.

TSUNAMI

The earthquake triggered tsunami waves. In just 30 minutes, the first wave hit the northeast coast. In less than an hour, the powerful, relentless waves had destroyed many coastal communities. They swept up cars,

ships, and houses, smashing them into bigger buildings and bridges. A 33-foot (10-meter) wave struck the city of Sendai, deluging the airport and farmland. Iwate, Miyagi, and Fukushima were the three areas hardest hit. More than 14,800 people died with a further 10,000 missing.

PACIFIC WARNINGS

The tsunami warning was extended across the Pacific. Hawaii and the Americas braced themselves, but when the waves came, they were no more than 8 feet (2.5 m) high.

Kisenuma city, Miyagi Prefecture, became a mass of debris and destruction.

NUCLEAR DISASTER

After the quake, the nuclear reactors at the Fukushima Nuclear Plant automatically shut down but the tsunami inundated the cooling systems causing a nuclear panic. By April 2011, a 19-mile (30-km) evacuation zone was still in force. High radiation levels were detected.

EYEWITNESS

According to the *Japan Times*, the Koganji Temple in Otsuchi was a designated evacuation site where only a week before there was a disaster preparedness drill. But, at only 0.6 miles (1 km) from the shore, it was engulfed by the waves. Deputy chief priest Ryokan Ogayu and his wife, Tomoko, lost their 19-year-old son and Tomoko's father-in-law. "We thought it was safe," said Tomoko.

SOMALIA

INDIA

THAILAND

INDIAN OCEAN

INDONESIA

Indian Ocean Tsunami, 2004

When the turquoise sea dramatically drained from Thailand's sun-soaked shoreline leaving fish gasping and tourists bemused, only a few recognized it as the ominous indicator of a tsunami. They shouted warnings, ran from the beach, and headed to higher ground. But there was scant time to issue alerts about the wall of water looming on the horizon.

The strange swelling of the sea gave little clue of the disaster about to unfold.

CHRISTMAS CATACLYSM

It was December 26, 2004, a date that now marks one of the world's worst natural catastrophes. When the water returned to Thailand's beaches, it came in such volume that it swept up everything in its path. Those who were not drowned risked injury in the massive amounts of debris whisked up by the waves, including boats and cars. It was sudden, shocking, and, for hundreds of thousands of people, fatal.

FROM ASIA...

Thailand was just one of many countries affected around the Indian Ocean. In Sri Lanka, the sea did not draw back, as it did in Thailand. It swelled immediately and immensely. There were no clues before its arrival and there was no mercy for the many coastal villages filled with people. The Indian state of Tamil Nadu likewise felt the full force of the disrupted ocean.

... TO AFRICA

Across the ocean in Somalia, East Africa, 176 people were killed and 50,000 left homeless. Even in South Africa, a death was reported in Port Elizabeth, and Durban harbor was closed due to the currents swirling around its mouth. Low-lying "paradise" isles, including the Maldives and the Andaman and Nicobar islands, were literally swamped.

... TO INDONESIA

The Indonesian islands suffered most, as these heavily populated islands were closest to the source of the disaster. Two months after the tsunami, bodies were still being found daily by the score. The recovery of the dead was expected to last for six months.

WHY DID IT HAPPEN?

An earthquake occurred off the west coast of Sumatra measuring 9.0 on the Richter scale. According to the U.S. Geological Survey, which monitors earthquakes around the world, the release of energy under the ocean was the equivalent to 23,000 Hiroshima-type atomic bombs. It was, quite simply, one of the largest earthquakes to shake the globe in a century. A further 15 quakes followed as two of the world's tectonic plates thrust against each other creating a rupture that measured 750 miles (1,200 km).

DEATH TOLL

No one will ever know the final death toll, although a figure of 310,000 is likely. Many of the dead were elderly or very young, often ripped from their families by the force of the water.

AFTERMATH

The aftermath in some coastal areas was like a nuclear holocaust. Most of the palm trees were, like homes, schools, and businesses, sucked up and spat out. Beneath the tangled mess were an unknown number of victims. Great swathes of Asia and the eastern rim of Africa turned from lush green to sludge brown in the moments it took for the water to flood inland.

Trees were felled and forests destroyed near Ban Nam Khen village in Thailand in December 2004.

After the disaster, wall displays of photographs helped to identify people lost or killed during the tsunami.

NIGHTMARE

Many survivors had lost family and searched in desperation for loved ones. Corpses mounted, food was scarce, water supplies were contaminated, and medical help was limited. Many roads were impassable and the loss of fishing vessels meant there was no work or food for some communities. Tourists left, causing financial hardship for those reliant on tourism for their livelihoods.

AID EFFORT

As television pictures flashed across the world, a relief effort on an unprecedented scale cranked into action. Aid agencies were quick to supply fresh water and shelter to avert disease. However, no amount of aid could help survivors overcome the mental anguish they endured.

LEARNING FROM DISASTERS

Although earthquakes cannot be predicted, tsunamis can and that is why a warning system was established in the Pacific in 1948. There was no such warning system in the Indian Ocean in 2004. In 2011, the innovative German-Indonesian Tsunami Early Warning System (GITEWS) became operational. With potentially only 20 minutes between an earthquake and a tsunami hitting the Indonesian coast, an advanced system of land, sea, and satellite instruments, plus ocean-floor sensors, react together to deliver speedy, trustworthy warnings to a threatened area.

Papua New Guinea Tragedy, 1998

On July 17, 1998, three mountainous waves pounded the northern coastline of Papua New Guinea, carrying away at least 2,500 people. According to Costas Synolakis, head of a team of researchers at the University of Southern California, it was "about double the worst overland flow that we had seen before."

This sand bar separates the Bismarck Sea from the Sissano lagoon. There is no trace left of the village that was once here.

EARTHQUAKE

The tremor that caused the tsunami measured 7.1 on the Richter scale—a strong but not unusual quake. Tremors of this size or bigger strike somewhere on the globe every three weeks or so. The earthquake occurred approximately 45 miles (70 km) from Vanimo on the northern coast of Papua New Guinea on the evening of July 17, 1998. No houses were destroyed by the earthquake itself, and people who lived only 10 miles (16 km) from the most devastated area said that the shaking was not particularly intense.

LANDSLIDE

According to the U.S. Geological Survey, the epicenter was 12 miles (19 km) off shore. A major aftershock followed, less than an hour later. Synolakis says that the earthquake itself could not have generated such a large wave. He believes that it triggered an underwater landslide somewhere along the submarine trench, just off the north coast, where the sea floor plunges steeply.

LOUD RUMBLINGS

Survivors reported hearing loud sounds before the first wave. Some described the noise as being like a low-flying jet plane or the woop-woop of a helicopter. Some went down to the beach to see what the sound was. There were other reports of a strong blast of air sweeping in from the sea.

 LEARNING FROM TSUNAMIS

The 1998 Papua New Guinea tsunami became one of the most studied. Few people believed that underwater landslides—or Submarine Mass Failures (SMFs)—could cause major tsunamis.

The huge loss of life prompted a major underwater geological investigation. The information gathered and the methods used have had a major impact on tsunami science.

WALL OF WATER

Survivors of the disaster describe seeing a wall of water barreling toward the shore. But unlike a normal wave with a crest, this tsunami was like a plateau of water, averaging 30 feet (9 m) high and extending 3 miles (4.8 km) from front to back. The leading wave arrived five to ten minutes after the earthquake. It swept over the shore at speeds of up to 12 mph (19 kph) for more than a minute before draining away, ready for the next wave, which followed several minutes later. There was a smaller third wave.

Survivors from Sissano Village, faces smeared with black paint as a symbol of mourning and wearing traditional headdresses, join a member of the Australian Army on the first anniversary of the disaster.

IMPACT

The tsunami was particularly devastating because it hit a vulnerable section of the north coast, where a wide strip of land separates the ocean from a lagoon, which itself was left by a tsunami in 1907. The families of fishermen living on this sand bar had no way to escape the waves. The water washed away all trace of their houses, sweeping many into the lagoon, or pulling them back out to sea.

SWEPT AWAY

The tsunami affected 10 villages. In places, no building within 1,650 feet (500 m) of the coast remained standing. The traditionally built houses were swept into the lagoon, along with people, alive and dead. Some ended up tangled in the mangrove trees on the other side of the lagoon.

RAPID RESPONSE

The international aid efforts were quick and effective. Medical and search-and-rescue teams from Australia and New Zealand arrived on the scene to help and treat survivors. Many had retreated inland, scared of more waves and stunned by the sudden devastation of their lives.

EYEWITNESS

Sebastian Alosi, an 8-year-old boy, came out of the mangrove jungle almost a week after being swept there by the wave. Having survived the tsunami, his injuries almost killed him. Australian army medics at the hastily erected field hospital at Vanimo had to amputate his left leg but they saved his life. The soldiers sent there to help the wounded felt they were "returning an old favor." The people of Papua New Guinea had helped Australian soldiers during World War II.

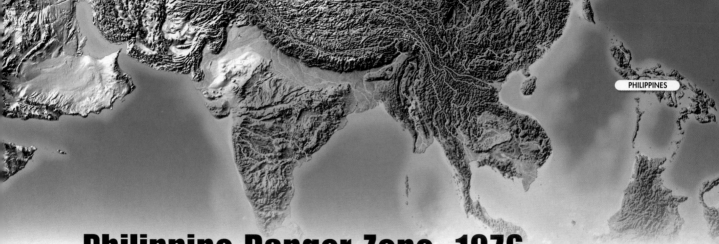

Philippine Danger Zone, 1976

A little after midnight on August 23, 1976, an earthquake measuring 8.0 on the Richter scale struck the southern Philippines. It lasted just 20 seconds and shook the coastal settlements of Alicia, Cotabato, Davao, and Pagadian City on the island of Mindanao, causing extensive damage. But it was the killer waves that came later that caused the biggest horror.

EPICENTER

The epicenter of the quake was beneath the Celebes Sea. The dazed residents of the coastal cities were just digging themselves out when the tsunami waves hit. The waves were 15 feet (4.5 meters) high. Up to 8,000 people died that night, mostly from drowning. Another 2,000 were injured and 90,000 made homeless.

PREVIOUS TSUNAMIS

In 1960, a 9.5 magnitude earthquake, the largest earthquake in recorded history, occurred in Chile. It generated massive tsunamis that traveled across the Pacific pounding the Philippines with waves up to 35 feet (10 m) high. And in 1572, the eruption of the Philippine volcano Taal on the central island of Luzon caused a tsunami in the lake from which the cone rises.

The Philippine Coast Guard examines "victims" during an earthquake and tsunami preparedness drill in Manila.

SEISMIC THREATS

There are two major fault lines in this area, the Sulu Trench in the Sulu Sea and the Cotabato Trench, a subduction zone where one tectonic plate is forced under another. Both faults are capable of producing major earthquakes and destructive local tsunamis. There are also a number of dangerous volcanoes.

 EYEWITNESS

For Dolores Obales, watching the devastation caused by the Japanese tsunami in 2011 brought back memories of the 1976 tsunami. She told the *Philippine Daily Inquirer* that she could recall the rumbling sound before the tsunami hit their village. She said nobody had any idea what the sound was until she heard her neighbors shouting, "Tidal wave, run, tidal wave is coming." She said, "The water in the shoreline receded before huge waves, about 10 feet (3 m) high, hit whatever was on their path."

Japan's Killer Wave, 1896

In 1896, there was no system to broadcast earthquake warnings, but for those who could read the signs on the east coast of Japan, there were clear indications of danger. On June 15, at around 7:30 PM, there was a series of long-lasting tremors. Twenty minutes later, the sea pulled back from the shore. A tsunami was on its way.

When it approached the shore, the wave was a mountain of water 100 ft (30 m) high and traveling at a phenomenal speed.

FESTIVITIES

The coastal towns of Sanriku province were packed with people celebrating a Shinto holiday with parades and pageants. Heavy rain had given way to clearer skies and so, when the tremors came, few took any notice. Earthquakes were commonplace.

DANGER

The long duration of the tremors told of a great submarine earthquake off shore. When the tide suddenly retreated, it left fish stranded and tore boats from their moorings. Out to sea there was a booming noise. As it grew louder, the revelers began to take notice but it was too late.

A FISHERMAN'S TALE

According to records of the time: "Of the entire population of the towns and villages that up to the moment of disaster were thriving with life, not one ... remained. On the other hand, the fishermen who at the time were some distance out at sea and had noticed nothing unusual were, on their way home the next morning, amazed to find the sea ... strewn with house wreckage and floating corpses."

SURVIVORS

A few escaped the wave. Some old men had gone up to the top of a cliff to escape the bustle of the festival. Some babies were saved by parents, who then returned for older children. Everyone else perished. The official death toll was 27,122.

WHY IT HAPPENED

Those at sea rarely notice a tsunami passing under them. The deadly wave may only be 2 feet (60 cm) high from crest to trough, but it is of usually miles long—and carries a great deal of water. This builds into a mountain when it is slowed by shallow water.

Krakatoa Catastrophe, 1883

The eruption of Krakatoa on August 27, 1883, was not unexpected. The three-cone volcano in the Sunda Strait between the Indonesian islands of Java and Sumatra had been active for some time. Indeed, the whole region was active. So, when the smallest cone started to rumble and release a vapor cloud, there was no great alarm.

MAKING AN ISLAND

Krakatoa was the remnant of a prehistoric volcano, some 6,000 feet (1,800 m) high, which had been blasted into dust. New outpourings of lava and ash piled up a new cone, which combined with two smaller cones to make Krakatoa Island. By 1883, it appeared to be extinct but, on May 20, the smallest of the three cones started thundering. "Booming sounds, like the firing of artillery," were heard.

CONCERNS

Activity then ceased only to resume on June 16. By the end of July the authorities were becoming concerned. Captain Ferzenaar of the Dutch colonial survey department went to Krakatoa to assess the situation. He found that the second largest cone had now opened. The island was stripped of vegetation and he advised against further visits.

ERUPTION

Then at 1 PM on Sunday, August 26, 1883, a series of massive explosions shook the island every 10 minutes or so. By 2 PM the vapor plume had reached 17 miles (27 km). By dusk the cloud had spread over an area of 125 square miles (320 square km). Lightning crackled around the cone, which emitted lethal, superheated gas, ash, cinder, stone, and mud into the Sundra Strait, setting off tsunamis.

Krakatoa is one of history's most famous volcanoes.

EYEWITNESS

On board the sailing ship *Charles Bal*, Captain W. J. Watson recorded in his log: "Chains of fire appeared to ascend and descend between the island and the sky. The blinding fall of sand and stones, the intense blackness above and around us, broken only by the incessant glare of varied kinds of lightning, and the continued explosive roars of Krakatoa, made our situation a truly awful one."

Krakatoa, Indonesia, 1883

TSUNAMIS

That evening, tsunamis caused death and devastation across the region. After each surge the water would recede, then return with even more force. Waves between 50 feet (15 m) and 130 feet (39 m) were recorded. The lighthouses along the Sunda Strait were toppled. Sebesi Island to the north of Krakatoa was completely submerged, drowning all its 3,000 inhabitants. By the time Merak, on the island of Java, was hit for the third time, the few survivors remaining were huddled in the stone houses at the top of a high cliff. The giant waves simply demolished them. Only two of the town's 3,000 residents survived.

Volcanic ash pours from Anak Krakatoa, "Krakatoa's Child."

CRESCENDO

The following morning, Krakatoa exploded with the loudest noise ever heard by human ears. The police chief on the island of Rodriguez 3,000 miles (4,800 km) away in the Indian Ocean said that the sound resembled, "the distant roar of heavy guns." The sound had taken four hours to get there. Exploding with the force of one million Hiroshima bombs, it blew debris into the air and covered an area larger than France with red-hot debris, ash and cinder. The vapor cloud rose 50 miles (80 km) into the air, casting a shadow over Southeast Asia. Dust in the atmosphere turned the sun blue and the sky red as far away as Trinidad.

TOTAL WIPEOUT

The tsunami washed away 300 settlements, clearing the shores of the Sunda Strait of human habitation. Some 36,000 people were killed. A giant wave damaged riverboats 2,000 miles (3,200 km) away in India and raised the tide in the English Channel, halfway round the world.

KRAKATOA'S CHILD

Only a tiny remnant of Krakatoa was still visible above the sea. Five months later, a researcher found spiders crawling across the island's ashy remains. Gradually vegetation returned. Then, in 1927, the caldera 900 feet (275 m) below the surface of the sea began to erupt again. In January 1928, Anak Krakatoa—Malay for Krakatoa's Child—emerged. The new cone is now over 1,000 ft (305 m) feet tall and still growing. Eruptions in January 2011 forced an evacuation of tens of thousands of people.

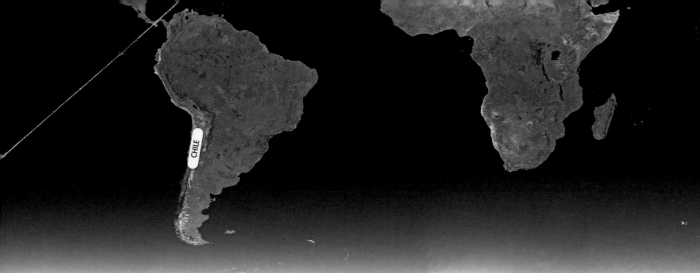

Giant Wave in Chile, 1868

In 1868, the USS *Wateree*, a two-masted steamship, came into the port of Arica near the Peru–Chile border. Her captain was seemingly aware that the area had a history of earthquakes and tsunamis, including one that had leveled the city of Concepción to the south in 1751. This awareness probably saved the crew's lives.

SHIPS IN PORT

On August 8, 1868, the *Wateree* was moored next to a Peruvian warship and an American merchant vessel when an earthquake struck. According to Lieutenant L.G. Billings who was on board the *Wateree*, the ship started to tremble. When he looked toward land, he saw a huge cloud of dust and heard a thundering noise that grew louder and louder.

EARTHQUAKE

As he watched, the hills seemed to move up and down, and then the cloud swallowed up the port. When the dust cleared, he was unable to believe what he saw: "Where a few seconds before there had stood a happy prosperous city, busy, active, and full of life, we saw nothing but ruins." An earthquake of approximately 9.0 magnitude had occurred off shore.

Nothing was left standing in Arica after the earthquake and tsunami flattened the town.

PRUDENCE

Even though the sea was calm, the Captain immediately put out to sea, worried about a possible tsunami. He set out extra anchors, closed the hatches and secured the guns on board. Back on land, survivors of the earthquake came down to the shore, calling to crews for help.

RESCUE PARTY

The *Wateree* sent out a yawl (a type of boat) with 13 men. Twelve men went ashore, while one stayed to man the boat. The rest of the crew prepared to send out a larger rescue party with tools and supplies.

EYEWITNESS

The crew of the *Wateree* heard a loud murmuring noise, which made them look up. Lieutenant Billings reported: "Looking toward the land we saw, to our horror, that where a moment before there had been a jetty, all black with human beings, there was nothing. Everything had been swallowed in a moment by the sudden rising of the sea, which the ship, floating upon it, had not noticed. At the same time we saw the yawl and its sailors carried away by the irresistible wave toward the lofty, vertical cliff of the Morro, where they disappeared in the foam as the wave broke against the rock."

SECOND QUAKE

An aftershock followed, and then the sea was suddenly sucked from underneath the *Wateree*. She was a flat-bottomed boat and so she just sat down on the seabed, whereas other ships with rounded hulls toppled on their sides. Fish floundered and other sea creatures were stranded. When the sea came back, it was as a huge tide. The *Wateree* lifted up, whereas those ships on their sides capsized.

This engraving shows the tidal wave hitting Arica, Chile, in 1868.

DEFYING PHYSICS

Lieutenant Billings said, "From that moment on, the sea seemed to defy all natural laws. Currents rushed in opposite directions, dragging us along at a speed that we could never have reached even if we had been going at full steam. The earth was still quaking at irregular intervals, but less violently and for shorter periods each time."

HUGE WAVE

After dark, the lookout warned of a breaking wave approaching the ship. The crew could see a thin phosphorescent line, which seemed to be rising higher and higher into the air. With a huge thunderous roar, the tsunami they had been dreading was upon them.

IMPACT

Lieutenant Billings said, "With a terrifying din, our ship was engulfed, buried under a half-liquid, half-solid mass of sand and water. We stayed under for a suffocating eternity. Then, groaning in all her timbers, our solid old *Wateree* pushed her way to the surface, with her gasping crew still hanging on the rails. A few men were seriously hurt. None was killed and nobody was missing." It was a miracle, but the wave swept her almost 2 miles (3 km) inland. The town of Arica was flattened. An estimated 25,000 were killed along the South American coast.

DISTANT SHORES

The tsunami spread across the Pacific, striking New Zealand and the Chatham Islands some 15 hours after the original earthquake, causing substantial damage.

EYEWITNESS

Billings said, "Out of Arica's ten or fifteen thousand inhabitants, a bare few hundred survived. For the three long weeks during which we waited for help, we shared the *Wateree*'s victuals and drinking water with these wretched people. I will not attempt to describe our feelings when at last we saw the United States Navy frigate *Powhatan*." Rescue and relief had finally arrived.

Arica looks like this today.

Lisbon Is Flattened, 1755

On the morning of November 1, 1755, Portugal was rocked by one of the most powerful earthquakes in recorded history. There was no accurate measuring equipment in those days, but scientists now believe the quake measured approximately 8.75 on the Richter scale. It was followed by two further tremors. People fled to the docks to escape the falling buildings, but then a cry went out: "The sea is coming; we shall all be lost."

ALL SAINTS' DAY

The first tremor occurred out in the Atlantic Ocean at around 9:40 AM. An eyewitness heard a sound "resembling the hollow distant rumbling of thunder." Most of the citizens of Lisbon were at church because it was All Saints' Day. They ran out and prayed for deliverance. It seemed to work. The trembling stopped. Then, suddenly, a second, more destructive shock hit the city, killing many people. Fifteen minutes later a third tremor hit the city. According to Portuguese eyewitness António Pereira: "The whole tract of country about Lisbon was seen to heave like the swelling of the billows in a storm." It destroyed 17,000 of the 20,000 buildings in the city.

After a terrible earthquake shook Lisbon, a giant tsunami devastated the area.

FIRE

The fact that this disaster had taken place on All Saints' Day only made things worse. Numerous candles toppled over, starting fires. A stiff northeasterly wind fanned the flames. Some buildings that had survived the tremors, such as the opera house, were suddenly on fire.

SAFETY

One of the survivors was a British merchant named Braddock. He managed to escape over the rubble and corpses to the banks of the Tagus River, where he thought he would be safe. Many people had the same idea. Then, an hour after the first tremor, the sea began to move out.

EYEWITNESS

Braddock wrote: "In an instant there appeared, at some small distance, a large body of water, rising as it were like a mountain. We all immediately ran for our lives, as fast as possible; many were actually swept away...

For my own part, I had the narrowest escape, and should certainly have been lost had I not grasped a large beam that lay on the ground, till the water returned to its channel, which it did almost in the same instant."

DEATH AND DESTRUCTION

The estimated death toll in Lisbon was 30,000, though estimates vary from 15,000 to 75,000. The earthquake affected a huge area. A fissure opened up in a small coastal village in Morocco killing about 8,000 people. Unusual sea waves were noted in England at 2 PM. Four hours later, a 24-foot (7-m) wave was seen in the Lesser Antilles, on the other side of the Atlantic.

This image shows Lisbon today. Rebuilding began within a year of the quake.

AFTEREFFECTS

In Lisbon the aftershocks continued. The King of Portugal had been out of Lisbon at the time of the earthquake. He returned and opened the palace kitchens to feed the survivors.

RESTORING ORDER

The King's chief minister, the Marquis de Pombal, stationed troops at the city gates to prevent the skilled workers needed to rebuild the city from leaving, and to stop looters. Gallows were erected and the corpses of 34 looters left hanging from them to deter others. Church approval was secured to bury the dead at sea, preventing the spread of disease.

KEEPING INFORMED

Pombal realized that accurate information was needed to calm people's fears. The local newspaper, *Gazeta de Lisboa*, never missed an issue. Ships were sent out to Portugal's empire to spread the word that Lisbon, a major trading center, was still open for business.

BACK TO BUSINESS

Through strong leadership, the great city of Lisbon was quick to react. Firefighting and demolition teams went to work. The homeless were housed in temporary accommodations and grain was sold by the government at pre-earthquake prices. No one was allowed to be thrown out of their homes and no one could charge rent. Timber was brought into the city and kilns were built at record speed to make new bricks.

LEARNING FROM CATASTROPHES

The Lisbon earthquake of 1755 was one of the first to be studied scientifically. Pombal sent questionnaires out to every parish in Portugal. He also worked with engineers on building the first ever earthquake resistant buildings. Elsewhere Italian scientists had made crude seismographs sometime before and, in 1760, an Englishman named John Michell published his theory that earthquakes were caused by "shifting masses of rock miles below the surface."

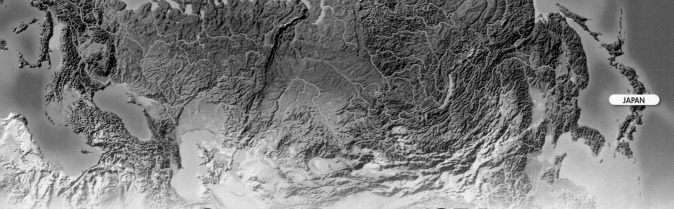

Japan's Sea of Terror, 1854

In the Gulf of Sagami, to the south of Tokyo, there is a fault in the earth's crust. It is an area of frequent earthquakes, but the one on December 23, 1854, caused a disastrous tsunami that destroyed more than 10,000 buildings and caused the death of over 2,000 people. The Russian frigate *Diana* was anchored in the harbor of Simoda on the Izu peninsula.

In this illustration, the wrecked frigate, Diana, is shown after the tsunami of 1854.

FIRST TREMOR

At 9:15 AM, there was a very strong tremor that lasted for two or three minutes. At 10 AM, a huge wave rushed into the bay and, within minutes, Simoda was underwater. The many ships anchored in the port were thrown against one another. Five minutes later, the water swelled and bubbled, washing mud, straw, and every kind of rubbish over the town.

THE *DIANA*

The officer on watch recorded the event. "At 11:15 AM the frigate dragged her anchors and lost one of them. Presently she lost the other and the ship was then whirled around and swept along with a strength that grew greater with ever-increasing speed.... The rise and fall of the water in this narrow bay was such that it caused several whirlpools, among which the frigate spun round with such force that in the midst of these gyrations, she turned clear round 43 times."

RISE AND FALL

The water continued to rise and fall for the next 45 minutes, with the swell ranging from 8 to 45 feet (2.5 to 14 m). The *Diana* struck the sea floor breaking off a part of her keel. Eventually the sea became calm.

EYEWITNESS

A second eyewitness account reported: "There was a great loss of life; many houses were washed into the sea, and many junks were carried up—one, two miles inland—and dashed to pieces on the shore. The bay was beautifully fine and no warning was given of the approaching convulsion. It was calm in the morning and the wind continued light all day." The next day, another earthquake of the same magnitude hit the region causing more death and destruction, but there was no accompanying tsunami.

Predicting Tsunamis

It is difficult to predict tsunamis because they are caused by other events. Early warning systems can spot events that may trigger a tsunami, or identify a tsunami when it is on its way. Sometimes there may be little time left for people to escape.

A high-tech buoy is placed off the coast of Sumatra as part of the Indian Ocean tsunami warning system.

TSUNAMI WARNING

Local early warning systems detect signs of earthquakes and can predict a possible tsunami. Sirens and public address systems then warn people of danger. There are many false alarms because it is not possible to tell whether a tsunami will actually occur. Remote warning systems are more accurate. They use wave gauges and sea-floor pressure gauges to spot a sudden rise in sea level or rise in pressure on the sea bed that means a tsunami has already started. The tsunami is then modeled by a computer and accurate predictions and warnings can be issued.

WATCHING FROM SPACE

The tsunami in the Indian Ocean in 2004 was the first spotted by satellite but it didn't help those affected. It took five hours to process the information and it was only by chance that the satellite was passing the area at the appropriate time. More usefully, satellites monitor the movement of tectonic plates and any telltale bulging of volcanoes. Warnings of the causes of tsunamis aid their detection.

Satellites in space help to monitor earth movement.

UP AGAINST THE WALL

Some places, such as Japan and the Maldives, have built strong sea walls in the hope of holding back a tsunami. Some experts believe that a strong tsunami could smash down these walls or simply sweep over the top. There is also a risk of people being crushed against the wall in the backwash.

TSUNAMI WARNING SYSTEMS

There are now a number of tsunami warning systems around the world, all coordinated through the International Tsunami Information Center in Hawaii. The Pacific Tsunami Warning Center has the responsibility of issuing warnings. It evaluates the potential tsunami risk using seismic data. If an earthquake occurs at sea at 60 miles (95 km) or less from the shore and above a certain magnitude, it will send a radio warning to the relevant tsunami warning centers by satellite. The warning is passed on to local emergency agencies by phone, radio, email, and the internet.

Looking to the Future

Seismology instruments are becoming increasing sophisticated, as are the tsunami early warning systems. The challenge for the future is to identify places that are in danger of a large tsunami and to supply warnings early enough for evacuations to take place. Getting relief to an area quickly is also paramount.

THE RISKS

Earthquake-prone regions are always at risk from tsunamis. Japan and the west coast of the Americas are in danger, not just from local quakes but also from ones traveling across the Pacific. Indonesia is likely to suffer more earthquakes and tsunamis. The Mediterranean could be in danger from an eruption of Mount Vesuvius in Italy, or a Greek island volcano.

A tsunami from the Canary Islands could sweep across the Atlantic and destroy New York.

MEGA-TSUNAMIS

A mega-tsunami is a giant tsunami, larger than any on record. The last known mega-tsunami was 4,000 years ago at Réunion Island in the Indian Ocean. The largest recorded wave was in Alaska in 1958, caused by a landslide. It was 1,600 feet (half a kilometer) high. Scientists think that when the volcano Cumbre Vieja in the Canary Islands erupts, a huge landslide may send a block of rock the size of a small island crashing into the Atlantic. A gigantic wave would race across the ocean and sweep away everything within 12 miles (20 km) of the coast in North America and the Caribbean.

Temporary homes on stilts house survivors of the tsunami in the Indian Ocean in 2004.

RELIEF EFFORTS

People struck by a tsunami need help immediately, and for months or years afterward. After the emergency services have rescued people who are trapped, injured, or drifting in the sea, the next job is to provide food, shelter, water, and medical help. Then the work of rebuilding lives and communities must begin.

 FROM OUTER SPACE

In the distant past, meteorites crashing into the sea may have caused some mega-tsunamis. Geological evidence suggests that large tsunamis hit the coast of Australia and New Zealand a few hundred years ago, probably caused by meteorites. Scientists predict there is a one in 300 chance of a huge meteorite, known as 1950 DA, hitting the earth on March 16, 2880. It could cause a tsunami 400 feet (120 m) high.

Timeline

November 1, 1755, Portugal
After one of the most powerful earthquakes in recorded history, a giant tsunami washed over the city of Lisbon, killing an estimated 30,000 people and destroying 17,000 of the 20,000 buildings.

December 23, 1854, Japan
A disastrous tsunami destroyed more than 10,000 buildings and caused the death of over 2,000 people on the Izu peninsula.

August 8, 1868, Chile
Nothing was left standing in Arica, Chile, after a large earthquake and the subsequent tsunami flattened the town.

August 1883, Indonesia
The monumental eruptions of Krakatoa caused tsunami waves up to 130 feet (39 m), which washed away 300 settlements. Some 36,000 people were killed. A wave destroyed boats as far away as India and raised the English Channel, halfway around the world.

June 15, 1896, Japan
A series of long-lasting tremors caused a tsunami 100 feet (30 m) high and traveling at phenomenal speed. Few escaped the wave in the coastal towns of Sanriku province.

April 1, 1946, Hawaii
An earthquake off the coast of Alaska triggered a tsunami that struck the Hawaiian Islands five hours later. It was as if the wave came from nowhere, with no warning.

July 9, 1958, Alaska

The largest recorded tsunami wave was caused by a landslide. It was 1,600 feet (half a kilometer) high.

August 23, 1976, Philippines
An 8.0 magnitude earthquake struck the southern Philippines. Dazed residents of the coastal cities were digging themselves out when tsunami waves hit. Up to 8,000 people died, mostly from drowning.

July 17, 1998, Papua New Guinea

An underwater landslide off the coast of Papua New Guinea is thought to have caused three mountainous waves to sweep over a strip of land, washing fishing villages into the lagoon beyond.

December 26, 2004, Indian Ocean
An earthquake off the coast of Indonesia caused one of the world's worst natural catastrophes in history. Tsunami waves barreled across the Indian Ocean, swamping communities in Indonesia, Thailand, Malaysia, Sri Lanka, India, and East Africa. More than 300,000 people lost their lives.

March 11, 2011, Japan
The Tohoku Earthquake off the northeast coast of Japan sent a catastrophic tsunami to destroy many coastal communities. It also flooded the Fukushima Nuclear Power Plant, causing a nuclear crisis.

Glossary

backwash The movement of water draining back to the sea after a wave has broken.

buoy A floating device, anchored to the sea floor, that often acts as a marker to show hazards under water.

crust The hard, outer layer of the earth.

debris Wreckage.

earthquake A sudden, violent shaking of the land caused by the movement of tectonic plates.

epicenter The point on the earth's surface that is directly above the place where an earthquake occurs.

fissure A long, narrow crack in the earth.

friction Resistance produced by two surfaces rubbing together as one tries to move over the other.

frigate A type of sailing warship.

geographical Relating to the features of the landscape.

geological Relating to rocks and minerals.

gyrations Quick, circular movements.

junks Flat-bottomed sailing boats typical in the Far East.

landslide A slippage of a large mass of rock or earth.

magma chambers A cavity in a volcano filled with red-hot, molten rock under extreme pressure.

magnitude The size or extent of something.

mangrove A type of tree that grows in flooded or very swampy land.

mantle A layer of the earth formed of semi-liquid, moving, molten rock.

meteorite A lump of rock, ice, or metal from space.

Minoan Relating to the Bronze Age culture of Crete that existed between 3000 and 1100 BCE.

phosphorescent Something that gives off light without heat.

Richter scale A scale for measuring the intensity of earthquakes.

seismic data Information gathered from studying earthquakes and other vibrations of the earth.

seismology The science relating to the study of earthquakes.

sonar Sound waves.

subduction zone Where an oceanic plate is forced under a continental plate.

submarine Existing under the sea.

tectonic plates Vast slabs of the earth's crust that carry the oceans and continents.

Further Information

FURTHER READING

Bonar, Samantha. *Tsunamis* (Natural Disasters). Mankato, MN: Capstone Press, 2006.

Cunningham, Kevin. *Surviving Tsunamis* (Perspectives: Children's True Stories: Natural Disasters). Chicago, IL: Heinemann-Raintree, 2011.

Lace, William W. *The Indian Ocean Tsunami of 2004* (Great Historic Disasters). New York, NY: Chelsea House Publishers, 2008.

Levy, Matthys and Mario Salvadori. *Earthquakes, Volcanoes, and Tsunamis: Projects and Principles for Beginning Geologists.* Chicago, IL: Chicago Review Press, 2009.

WEB SITES

Due to the changing nature of Internet links, Rosen Publishing has developed an online list of Web sites related to the subject of this book. This site is updated regularly. Please use this link to access this list:

http://www.rosenlinks.com/cata/tsun

DVDs

The Day After Tomorrow directed by Robert Emmerich (2004)
Krakatoa, East of Java directed by Bernard L. Kowalski, director. (1969)
National Geographic: Tsunami— Killer Wave (2005)

Index